Planets

Saturn

Dash!
LEVELED READERS
An Imprint of Abdo Zoom • abdobooks.com

3

Dash!
LEVELED READERS

Level 1 – Beginning
Short and simple sentences with familiar words or patterns for children who are beginning to understand how letters and sounds go together.

Level 2 – Emerging
Longer words and sentences with more complex language patterns for readers who are practicing common words and letter sounds.

Level 3 – Transitional
More developed language and vocabulary for readers who are becoming more independent.

abdobooks.com

Published by Abdo Zoom, a division of ABDO, PO Box 398166, Minneapolis, Minnesota 55439. Copyright © 2019 by Abdo Consulting Group, Inc. International copyrights reserved in all countries. No part of this book may be reproduced in any form without written permission from the publisher. Dash!™ is a trademark and logo of Abdo Zoom.

Printed in the United States of America, North Mankato, Minnesota.
092018
012019

Photo Credits: iStock, NASA, Science Source, Shutterstock
Production Contributors: Kenny Abdo, Jennie Forsberg, Grace Hansen, John Hansen
Design Contributors: Dorothy Toth, Neil Klinepier

Library of Congress Control Number: 2018946203

Publisher's Cataloging in Publication Data

Names: Murray, Julie, author.
Title: Saturn / by Julie Murray.
Description: Minneapolis, Minnesota : Abdo Zoom, 2019 | Series: Planets | Includes online resources and index.
Identifiers: ISBN 9781532125317 (lib. bdg.) | ISBN 9781641856768 (pbk) | ISBN 9781532126338 (ebook) | ISBN 9781532126840 (Read-to-me ebook)
Subjects: LCSH: Saturn (Planet)--Juvenile literature. | Saturn (Planet)--Ring system--Juvenile literature. | Planets--Juvenile literature. | Saturn (Planet)--Exploration--Juvenile literature.
Classification: DDC 523.46--dc23

Table of Contents

Saturn 4

Amazing Rings 16

Missions to Saturn 18

More Facts 22

Glossary 23

Index 24

Online Resources 24

Saturn

Sun

Mercury

Earth

Venus

Saturn is the sixth planet from the sun. The massive planet is the second largest in our **solar system**.

Titan

6

Saturn has 62 known moons. Titan is its largest moon. It is bigger than the planet Mercury! Scientists believe there are many more moons to be discovered around Saturn.

It takes Saturn 29.5 Earth years to **orbit** the sun. As it orbits, it also spins. It takes 10 hours and 42 minutes to complete one rotation. This time is equal to one day on Saturn.

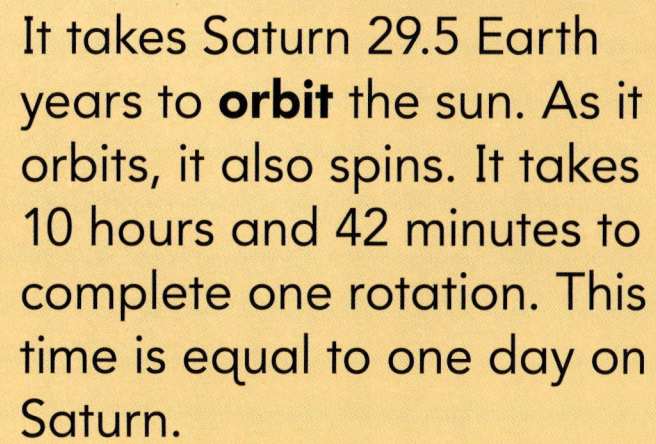

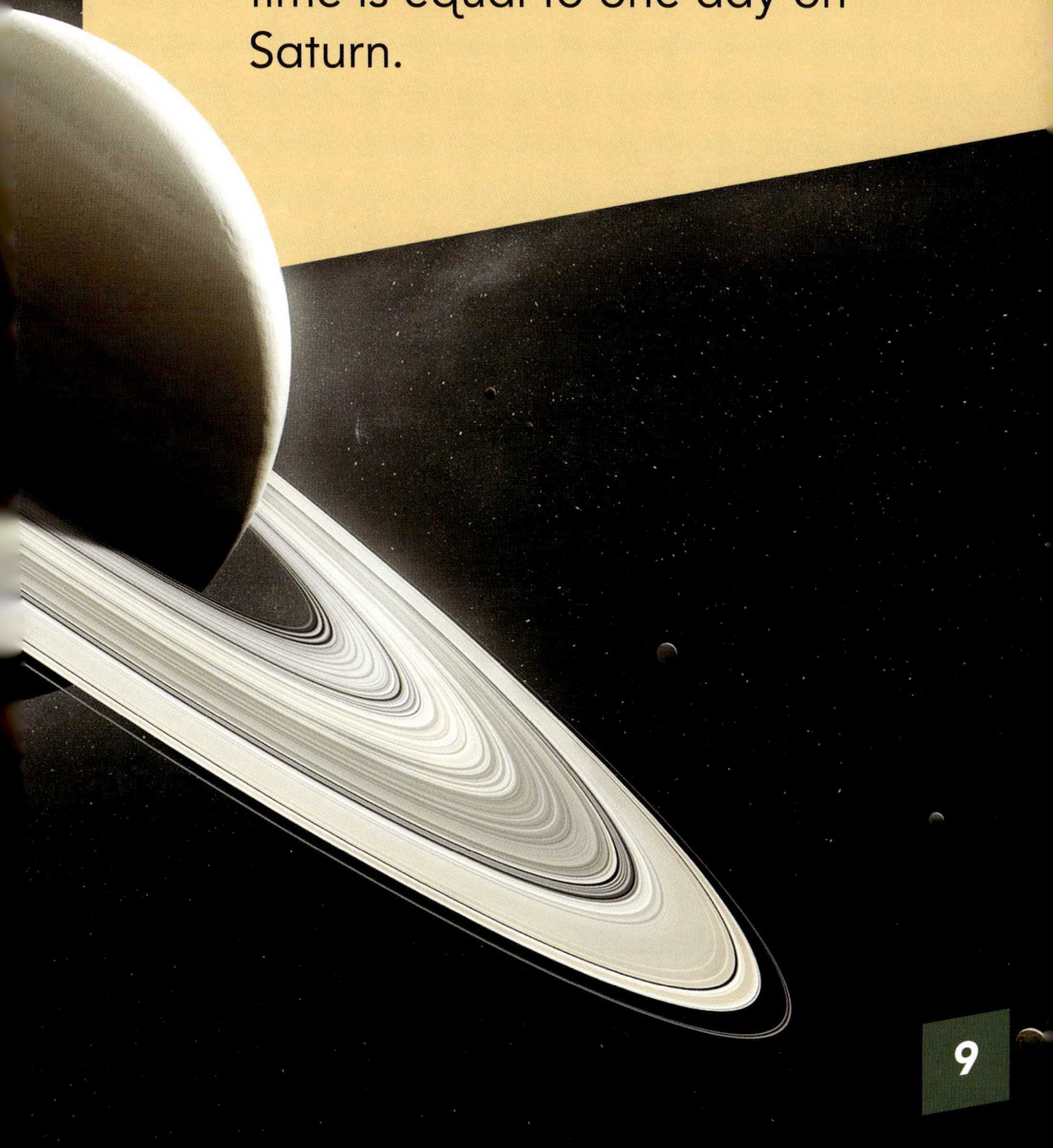

Saturn has no solid surface. It is made up of gas and liquid. The **atmosphere** consists mainly of hydrogen and helium. The planet appears pale yellow in color.

Saturn's extremely hot core is made up of iron and rock. Temperatures can reach 21,000 °F (11,648 °C)! Saturn's middle layer consists of liquid and gases.

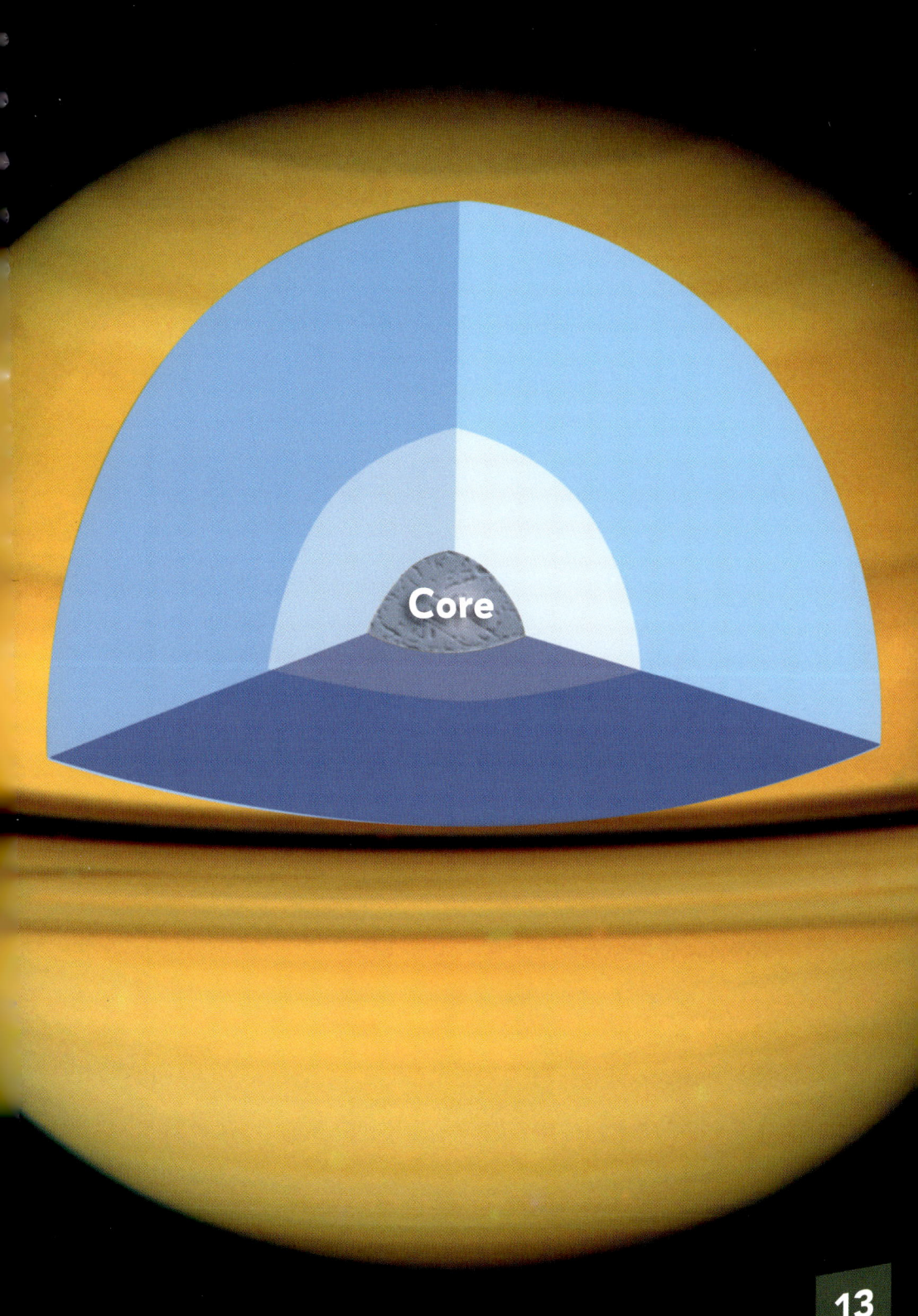

Saturn's average temperature is -178 °F (-116.7 °C). Winds can reach more than 1,000 mph (1,609 kph). Big storms swirl around the planet. A cloud pattern shaped like a hexagon has sat over Saturn's north pole for many years.

Amazing Rings

16

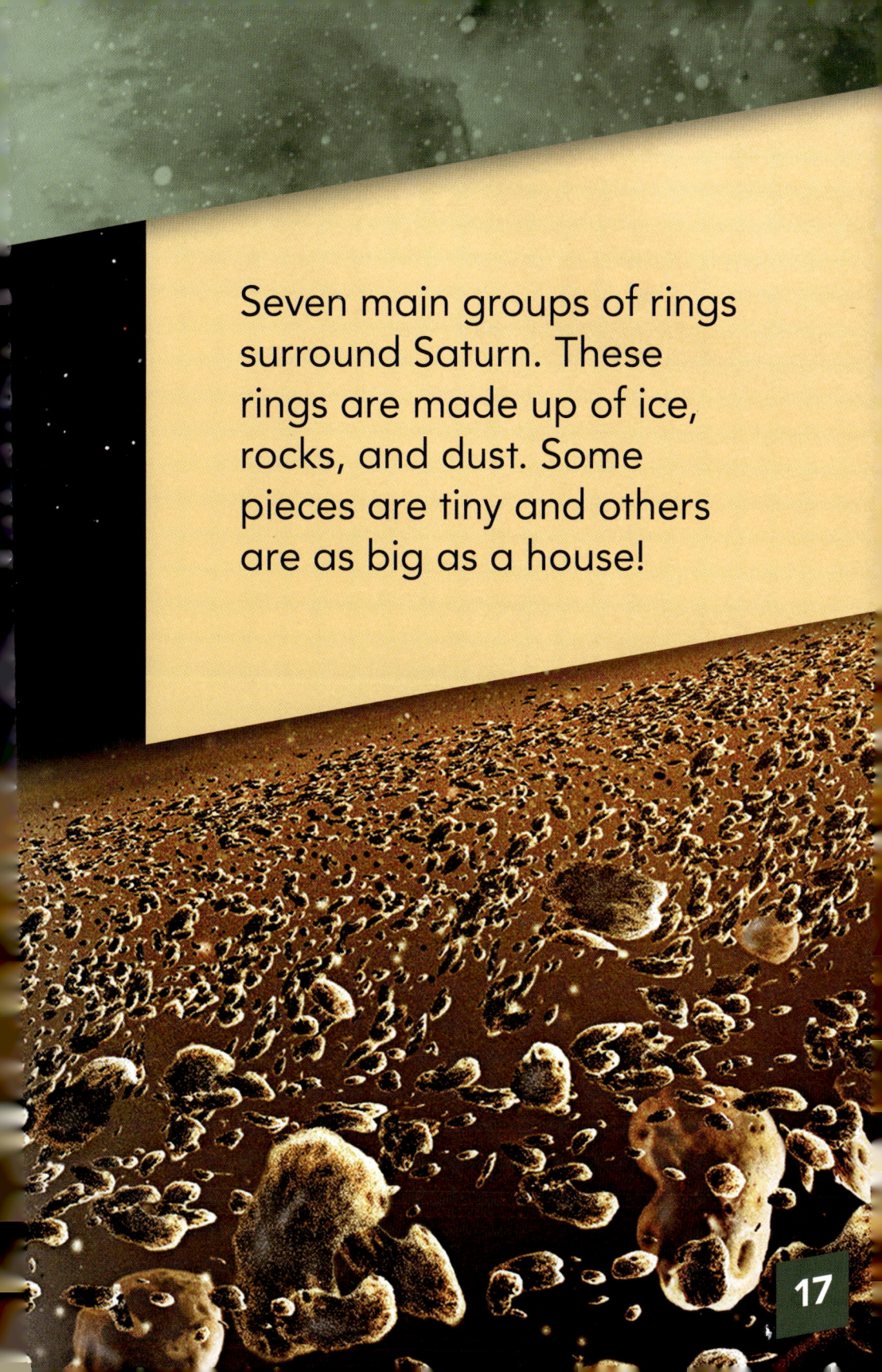

Seven main groups of rings surround Saturn. These rings are made up of ice, rocks, and dust. Some pieces are tiny and others are as big as a house!

Missions to Saturn

There have been four space missions to Saturn. Pioneer 11 flew by the planet in 1979. In 1980 and 1981, Voyager 1 and 2 were able to gather information on the planet's rings and moons.

The *Cassani–Huygens* mission went into Saturn's **orbit** in 2004. It discovered new moons and new details of the planet's rings. The *Huygens* **probe** landed on Titan in 2005. It sent back amazing photos of the moon's surface!

More Facts

- Saturn is so big that more than 760 Earths could fit inside the planet.

- Saturn is the least dense planet. If placed in a tub of water, it would float on the top.

- Saturn's rings span out 175,000 miles (281,635 km) from the planet.

Glossary

atmosphere – the gases surrounding the earth or other planets in our solar system.

orbit – a curved path in which a planet, or other space object, moves in a circle around another body.

probe – an unmanned, exploratory spacecraft designed to transmit information about its environment.

solar system – a system that includes a star (the sun) and all of the matter which orbits it, including planets and their moons.

Index

atmosphere 11

color 11

composition 11, 12

day 9

Mercury 7

missions 18, 20

moons 7, 18, 20

rings 17, 18, 20

size 5

sun 5

Titan (moon) 7, 20

Voyager 1 18

weather 14

year 9

Online Resources

To learn more about Saturn, please visit **abdobooklinks.com**. These links are routinely monitored and updated to provide the most current information available.